How to Read a THiNKaha® Book
A Note from the Publisher

The THiNKaha series is the CliffsNotes of the 21st century. The value of these books is that they are contextual in nature. Although the actual words won't change, their meaning will change every time you read one as your context will change. Experience your own "aha!" moments ("AhaMessages™") with a THiNKaha book; AhaMessages are looked at as "actionable" moments—think of a specific project you're working on, an event, a sales deal, a personal issue, etc. and see how the AhaMessages in this book can inspire your own AhaMessages, something that you can specifically act on. Here's how to read one of these books and have it work for you.

1. Read a THiNKaha book (these slim and handy books should only take about 15–20 minutes of your time!) and write down one to three actionable items you thought of while reading it.

2. Mark your calendar to re-read this book again in 30 days.

3. Repeat step #1 and write down one to three more AhaMessages that grab you this time. I guarantee that they will be different than the first time. BTW: this is also a great time to reflect on the actions taken from the last set of AhaMessages you wrote down.

After reading a THiNKaha book, writing down your AhaMessages, re-reading it, and writing down more AhaMessages, you'll begin to see how these books contextually apply to you. THiNKaha books advocate for continuous, lifelong learning. They will help you transform your ahas into actionable items with tangible results until you no longer have to say "aha!" to these moments—they'll become part of your daily practice as you continue to grow and learn.

As the Chief Instigator of Ahas at THiNKaha, I definitely practice what I preach. I read *Alexisms* and *Ted Rubin on How to Look People in the Eye Digitally*, and one new book once a month and take away two to three different action items from each of them every time. Please e-mail me your ahas today!

Mitchell Levy
publisher@thinkaha.com

D1598385

Dedication

For Jerry Porter and Barbara Croft Porter, whose humanity, support, and friendship have proven invaluable.

Acknowledgments

Thank goodness these acknowledgments need not be limited by the length of a tweet.

Jerry and Barbara Porter have been through every sentence of the various revisions, being continually helpful and supportive as they always are. My valuable and always available coach, Jen Zobel Bieber, is a sensitive, sensible, and reliable sounding board for everything I write. I have relied on my administrative assistant, Elaine Murrin, not only for organization and text support but also for her discerning taste in artwork.

My extraordinary sisters, Emily Lipof and Sheila Schwartz, are those without whom I could not have done, especially in recent years. My admirable son, Alexander Gopen, is continually a special light in my life. I have relied on the advice and reactions and support of all three.

Annie Wormhoudt, Kristy Murray, and Alan Alda were all kind enough to be early readers for the project. Annie was present at a four-hour dinner one remarkable fall evening in Silicon Valley at the Information Development World conference with me and Mitchell Levy, the creator of the Aha Amplifier, during which Mitchell hornswoggled me into trying my hand at generating 140 tweets on my take on the English language. I consider Mitchell the book's Prime Mover and Annie the book's godmother.

My thanks to Jenilee Maniti, who from half a world away oversaw all the production matters with the greatest of competence.

In memoriam: Whenever I present Reader Expectations to a new public, I always gratefully recognize Joe Williams, Greg Colomb, and Frank Kinahan, my partners in the firm Clearlines, 1980-1990, with whom many of the seeds for these ideas were planted.

Also in memoriam: My sense of the way language functions owes its beginnings to my really wonderful piano teacher, Miss Esther Hewes, with whom I studied from age seven to eighteen. I still see the quiet smile that accompanied her saying, "Now, we didn't get that quite right, did we?"

Contents

A Two-Part Prologue

The generation of this book is a striking example of serendipity in action. In September of 2015, I attended Scott Abel's annual conference, Information Development World. I knew no one there, even though I was to be one of the keynote speakers. At the Presenter's Happy Hour, after all forty of us had introduced ourselves to the group as a whole, we informally broke up into groups of four or five people to chat while enjoying a free glass of wine. Most of these groups immediately engaged in lively conversation, suggesting that they were old acquaintances, happy to re-encounter one another. I looked for a quiet, unenthusiastic group, presumably made up of people who had never before or had just barely met each other. There was only one of these. That is how I met Mitchell Levy. When the wine was gone, signaling the end of the festivities, Mitchell and I were the only ones left in our group. I suggested we dine together. The result was this book.

Mitchell explained how he was publishing a series of books made up of 140 tweets, each devoted to a single subject. The format raised a double challenge: (1) The 140 tweets must be able to be read from beginning to end as a cohesive and coherent whole; and (2) each tweet had to be able to stand by itself, making inter-referentiality impossible. He challenged me to do this for my unusual—indeed, radical—new way of analyzing and controlling the English language. (I call it the Reader Expectation Approach.) While presuming the task would prove impossible for my material, I agreed to try my hand at the process later in the evening.

By the morning, I had generated twenty. I could imagine another twenty, but not another 100 to follow. Mitchell and I dined again the following evening. He is a persuasive fellow—energetic, articulate, and witty. I told him I couldn't see pushing aside the many important tasks on my desk to experiment with this further; but since I happened to be taking six flights, some of them long ones, in the next three weeks, I succumbed to his energy and promised to devote my air travel time to the project. By the time I landed for the sixth time, I had generated 142 of these encomia, these linguistic-rhetorical proverbs, all at 30,000 feet. I was hooked. The entire experiment has been a joy. I recommend it to anyone who has 140 things to say about their most passionate interest.

****

I think we have been teaching writing badly for the entire 250 years we've been battling with the problem. Because we teach it to kids, we teach it at the lowest of intellectual levels. The resulting rules fail to work well for adults engaged in professional worlds. We assign students tasks that no busy adult would ever be willing to perform: "Fill these pages exclusively for the purpose of our being able to evaluate how well you can fill pages which otherwise need not be filled." The students are writing for a fearsome audience: the big red pen in the sky. They are writing for an audience (the teacher) who they think knows everything that can be known about the subject at hand and therefore has no need to read. Students have an artificial rhetorical task: They do not write to *communicate* what they know to someone who has a need to know (which is what professionals are constantly doing); instead, they write to *demonstrate* to Teacher that they have done their assignment. That task of demonstration is far more easily accomplished (and therefore far more boring) than is the communication task. All you have to do is find stuff on the Internet (no longer even in the "lie-bury") and spread it around on the page. Teacher will know how to connect the dots. And Teacher does.

We have always considered the teaching of writing from the perspective of looking over the shoulder of the writer, announcing what can or cannot, must or must not, should or should not be done in the presence of a cultivated society. In school, we credit students for working hard and for improving since last time. But in the world of adult professionals, no one cares about these manifestations of effort. In that world, the important person where writing is concerned is not the writer; it is the reader. The only question of importance is whether the reader got delivery of what the writer was trying to send. That's it. If delivery was made, the writing was good enough; if not, it wasn't.

So I undertook the task, back in 1980, of figuring out how readers go about making sense of writing. Thirty-six years later, I am completely convinced that readers take the vast majority of their clues for interpretation not from word choice nor from word meaning, but instead from the structural location of words. We know *where* in a sentence to look for certain kinds of *substance*. That knowledge breeds what I call Reader Expectations. Once you know *where* readers expect to find *what*, you can manipulate your sentence structure so the right words appear in the right places. That, in turn, will control most of your readers' interpretive processes.

There are five major questions to which we as readers must have the correct answers at the end of every sentence if we are to get from that sentence what the writer wanted us to get:

- What's happening?

- Whose story is it?

- How does this sentence connect backward to its predecessor?

- How is this sentence leaning forward to where we might go from here?

- What are the most important words in this sentence—the ones we should be reading with extra emphasis?

If you as a reader get any one of these wrong, you cannot get what the writer intended you to get. The new news from the Reader Expectation Approach is this: We as readers have relatively fixed expectations of where in the structure of a sentence to find the answers to all five of these questions. If you know about those locations, you can use that knowledge to structure your sentence, which in turn will control much of your readers' interpretive processes. They will get what you were trying to send. In the process, it will lead you back into your thought process to discover if you have yet completely considered what it was you were trying to say.

Of course, this new approach cannot be adequately explained in 140 tweets. But I hope you can get enough of a taste of the matter that you will seek out lengthier expositions, either from articles posted on my website (www.GeorgeGopen.com) or from my two full-length books, *Expectations* and *The Sense of Structure*.

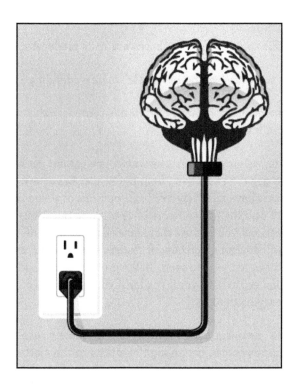

Section 1
In General

I once sat behind two students on a cross-campus bus who were discussing the big party that night at the frat house. One asked the other, "How can you go? You've got that paper due tomorrow for History." He responded, "I've done all the work. Now I just have to write it." Most of us were taught to assemble our materials, perhaps in a detailed outline form, after which the last task – "the writing" – was merely to transform all that stuff into error-free prose. In the real world (the world you live in after the last time you graduate), writing is an integral part of the thinking process. You don't know what you mean till you see what you say. People "know" you from your writing. Writing well is important.

1

The eyes are the windows to the soul.
One's writing is the window to one's mind.
@GeoGopen

_____

_____

_____

2

Most people feel their writing does not
adequately convey the power of their mind.
@GeoGopen

_____

_____

_____

3

Write well, because you will be known to many important people in your life only through your writing. @GeoGopen

_____

_____

_____

4

Writing is not what you do after the thinking process has concluded. It is part and parcel of the thinking process. @GeoGopen

_____

_____

_____

Section II
Quality and Style

A piece of writing is in the business of delivery. If it successfully transfers to the reader's mind the thoughts that were in the writer's mind, it is good writing. Quality is to be judged by the success of the attempted delivery.

Your writing style is the result of how you habitually go about forming sentences and paragraphs. Your style proclaims to readers who you are. Merely being error-free doth not a style make.

5

Bottom-line question regarding the quality of a piece of writing: Did the reader receive what the writer was intending to send? @GeoGopen

_____

_____

_____

6

If the reader perceived what the writer meant to communicate, then the writing was good enough; if not, not. @GeoGopen

_____

_____

_____

7

In the real world, where writing is concerned, the important person is not the writer; it is the reader. @GeoGopen

_____

_____

_____

8

In the real world – unlike in school – no one cares how hard the writer tried nor if the writer has improved since last time. @GeoGopen

_____

_____

_____

9

Quality of writing depends not on how much it impresses, but only on whether it succeeded in delivering the message to the reader. @GeoGopen

---

10

Good prose is always moving forward – from capital letter to period, and from one sentence to the next. @GeoGopen

---

11

Once your reader moves backward within or from a sentence, for any reason, you've lost control of your reader. @GeoGopen

_____

_____

_____

12

Where writing is concerned, style is choice. Where anything is concerned, style is choice. @GeoGopen

_____

_____

_____

13

Your personal writing style is the sum total of all the choices you habitually make when forming sentences and paragraphs. @GeoGopen

_____

_____

_____

14

Good prose should always be at least as well written as good poetry. @GeoGopen

---

15

Prose and music both "mean" by fulfilling and violating our expectations of where the next moment will take us. @GeoGopen

---

Section III
Expectations: Location, Location, Location

Rhetoric and real estate have this in common: The three most important things are location, location, and location. The most important contribution the Reader Expectation Approach makes to the understanding and control of writing is this: Readers take the great majority of their clues for making sense of a sentence not from what the words are nor from what they might mean, but rather from where in the sentence they show up. At the end of reading every sentence, we have to know what has happened, whose story it has been, how this sentence connects backward and forward to its neighbors, and which of its words are the most important – the stars of the show. Remarkably, as readers we know where within that sentence to look for the answers to those questions. As a writer, if you know those locations, and constantly place the right answers in the right places, you will successfully lead your readers directly to your thought. Your prose should be the stairway they climb to arrive at your meaning.

16

Context controls meaning. @GeoGopen

17

Where a word appears in a sentence will control most of the use to which that word will be put. @GeoGopen

_____

_____

_____

18

Nothing is more crucial in the effort to control writing than knowing what readers expect to find where in a sentence. @GeoGopen

_____

_____

_____

19

Expectation is a primary component
– perhaps *the* primary component – of
meaning in English. It may be so for all
languages. @GeoGopen

_____

_____

_____

20

The English language functions on the basis of whether a reader's expectations are fulfilled and/or violated at any given moment. @GeoGopen

_____

_____

_____

21

When writers learn how readers make sense of prose, writers can influence the reading process so most people will understand them. @GeoGopen

_____

_____

_____

22

Meaning is conveyed only partly (15%) by word choice and word meaning and 85% by the structural location of words. @GeoGopen

_____

_____

_____

23

Readers value the end of a sentence the most, the beginning a lot, and the middle so little it pales by comparison. @GeoGopen

_____

_____

_____

24

If you can control the beginnings and ends of sentences, providing readers with what they need there, then you're a good writer. @GeoGopen

_____

_____

_____

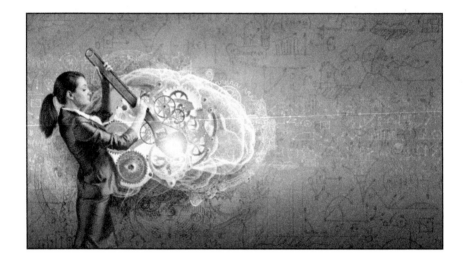

Section IV
The Interpretive Act

In school, students' writing is judged on two criteria: (1) Did the student produce enough of the right answers to the question posed by the assignment? 1492? Ocean blue? Christopher Columbus? (2) Was the writing free of errors and awkwardness? You get an A. The whole process is a kind of examination.

Not so in the real world. There the writer has to struggle to control what sense readers might make of the prose. So far are those readers from the teacher-like state of knowing the answers in advance, they must use all the clues you can give them to discover what thoughts had been coursing through your brain. The reader's interpretive act is complicated and hard for the writer to control. But the writer will do a better job of it if the writer understands what readers expect to find where. This knowledge provides the tools for mind control.

25

Readers read from left to right and through time. Writers should understand that and use it to their advantage. @GeoGopen

_____

_____

_____

26

Major problem: Every word unit (phrase, sentence, pgph.) is infinitely interpretable. Infinity = one more is always possible.
@GeoGopen

_____

_____

_____

27

You cannot write a sentence that will mean exactly the same to all readers. Complete control by the writer is impossible.
@GeoGopen

_____

_____

_____

28

Problem: Once you give your text to a reader, it's the reader's. In your absence, the reader will do whatever the reader will do. @GeoGopen

_____

_____

_____

29

When you are reading a word, you are reading it simultaneously as a part of multiple units – phrase, sentence, ... document. @GeoGopen

---

30

To read a sentence, one uses a single breath of "reader energy" to figure out, simultaneously, its structure and substance. @GeoGopen

---

31

It is insufficient to form a sentence that merely can be interpreted to mean what you want it to mean. @GeoGopen

32

A sentence must not only contain all the correct info; it must convince 95% of its readers how to read and interpret that info.
@GeoGopen

_____

_____

_____

33

Every word in a sentence should be able to perform some helpful function at the moment of its arrival. @GeoGopen

_____

_____

_____

34

When a student's writing is inadequate, teachers are often mistaken to think they know what the student intended to say. @GeoGopen

_____

_____

_____

35

Students write not for a "real" audience, but rather for someone they consider "the big red pen in the sky." @GeoGopen

_____

_____

_____

36

Students feel, with good reason, that they are writing for a reader who already knows everything the student might find to say. @GeoGopen

----

37

With teachers as their sole readers, students write not to communicate but only to demonstrate they have done their work. @GeoGopen

----

38

School writing assignments: "Fill these pages so we can evaluate how well you can fill pages that otherwise need not be filled."
@GeoGopen

_____

_____

_____

Section V
Bad Advice

I am sorry to say that almost all the standard pieces of advice we get on writing are either flawed or just plain wrong. The two most commonly given are "to make it better, make it shorter," and "avoid the passive." The first is flawed; the second is just plain wrong. Sentence length, by itself, has no relationship to quality. I can show you 13-word sentences that are completely opaque and 130-word sentences that read clear as a bell. The passive? Writers on any serious subject cannot do without it. In a book like this, I can only suggest that some advice is really, really bad. To explain why takes more space than is allowed by tweets. I've written two longer books that explore these matters at some length. If you don't somehow shake free from the traditional bad advice, it will often leave you helpless in a sea of thought.

39

Bad advice: "Write the way you speak." When you speak, you use body and voice to convey meaning. These disappear on paper. @GeoGopen

_____

_____

_____

40

Bad advice: "To see if your document is good, read it aloud." You already know how to read it. Will your reader? @GeoGopen

---

41

Terrible advice: "Avoid the passive." You cannot write sophisticated prose on a complex matter without the aid of the passive. @GeoGopen

42

The worst advice: "Avoid the passive" is the single worst piece of advice almost universally given concerning writing. @GeoGopen

_____

_____

_____

43

Useless advice: "Omit needless words." On some level, you thought you needed all those words. @GeoGopen

_____

_____

_____

44

Useless advice: "Omit needless words." There are many readerly "needs" that do not depend merely on logic. @GeoGopen

_____

_____

_____

45

Inadequate advice: "A paragraph's first sentence must be a Topic Sentence" doesn't work for writers in the professional world. @GeoGopen

_____

_____

_____

46

Bad advice made good: When a sentence exceeds 29 words, it does not become harder to read; it only becomes harder to write. @GeoGopen

_____

_____

_____

47

Rulish advice: Aside from the rules of grammar, there should be only one rule for writing: No Rules. @GeoGopen

_____

_____

_____

Section VI
The Passive

The advice to "avoid the passive" can be found in most books on writing. Pick up any of them (even the most famous ones), find this piece of advice, turn the page, and count the number of passives you find there. You will most likely find some. Look at Strunk and White's well-loved *Elements of Style*. In the 362 lines of their chapter on how to write well (which includes their advice to avoid the passive), they use the passive 38 times. We cannot do without the passive, if we are to make sense to our readers.

What does the passive do? It re-arranges the furniture. "Jack loves Jill" becomes "Jill is loved by Jack." Jack and Jill occupy different locations in the two sentences. What is the most important concern in writing? – location. If you need to get Jill up to the front of the sentence so she can occupy the right location for her within this thought, and the passive is the only way to do it, thank goodness for the passive. It should be given the green light.

48

The passive is not only OK; it is better than the active in all situations in which the passive does a better job than the active. @GeoGopen

_____

_____

_____

49

Good passive: If it is the only way to get to the front of a sentence the words that link it to the previous sentence. @GeoGopen

_____

_____

_____

50

Good passive: If it is the only way to make the grammatical subject state whose story the sentence is. @GeoGopen

_____

_____

_____

51

Good passive: If it is the only way to get the most important information next to a colon, semi-colon, or period. @GeoGopen

_____

_____

_____

52

Good passive: The best way to get rid of agency: "Jack loves Jill" –> "Jill is loved by Jack" –> "Jill is loved." @GeoGopen

_____

_____

_____

53

Theological argument for the passive: God would not have invented the passive if there weren't a good reason for it. @GeoGopen

_____

_____

_____

54

Darwinian argument for the passive: The passive would not have survived this long if it were not fit for something. @GeoGopen

_____

_____

_____

Section VII
Controlling How Readers Read Your Narrative

Reader Expectations are unconscious on the part of readers. They don't know that they read a sentence as being the story of the grammatical subject. They don't know that they look forward to the verb's telling them what actions are going on. But since they do these things, you, as writer, can control their narrative progress through your sentences by ensuring that they always know whose story it is and what actions are taking place. You can accomplish that by making the subject whose story it is and making the verb the action that is taking place. You will be guiding them through your narrative just as surely as if you had paved a path for them and surrounded it by a metallic trellis.

55

Readers read a clause as being the story of whoever or whatever shows up as its grammatical subject. @GeoGopen

_____

_____

_____

56

"Jack loves Jill" is the story of Jack. "Jack" is a context from which all the rest of the information proceeds. @GeoGopen

_____

_____

_____

57

"Jill is loved by Jack" is the story of Jill. If the passive is needed to get her up front, thank goodness we have the passive. @GeoGopen

_____

_____

_____

58

A reader reads a multi-clause sentence as being the story of who or what shows up as the grammatical subject of the main clause. @GeoGopen

_____

_____

_____

59

To see the stories readers perceive in your paragraph, circle all the grammatical subjects and read them in progression.
@GeoGopen

_____

_____

_____

60

Readers of English expect the action of a sentence to be articulated by its verb.
@GeoGopen

_____

_____

_____

61

If your verb says what's going on and your subject says who did it, your story will be clear to most readers. @GeoGopen

_____

_____

_____

62

There are no "weak verbs" or "strong verbs":
The weakness or strength depends on the
context in which the verb is found.
@GeoGopen

63

A verb is "weak" if its meanings have little or nothing to do with the action of the sentence as a whole. @GeoGopen

_____

_____

_____

64

A verb is "strong" if one of its meanings is the focal point of the action of the sentence as a whole. @GeoGopen

_____

_____

_____

65

To see the actions readers perceive in your paragraph, circle all the verbs and read them in progression. What you wanted?
@GeoGopen

_____

_____

_____

66

State as early as possible in a sentence the words that logically connect this sentence back to the one that preceded it.
@GeoGopen

_____

_____

_____

67

A sentence connects most easily to the one before it by providing a link backward either to its predecessor's beginning or end. @GeoGopen

_____

_____

_____

68

A reader will logically connect a sentence to its predecessor as soon as something in the new sentence can be connected backwards.
@GeoGopen

_____

_____

_____

69

A sentence must connect backward and forward to its neighbors as smoothly as a fine sentence flows from its start to its end.
@GeoGopen

_____

_____

_____

Section VIII
The Stress Position

The existence of the Stress position is the greatest unrevealed fact about the English language. Think of it this way: Wouldn't it be wonderful if we could print the words we wanted the reader to stress in red? Then no one (with the exception of a few color-blind males) would ever mistake which words we wanted emphasized. The powers that be won't let us do this; but we have something equally as effective – the Stress position.

You create a Stress position whenever the grammatical structure of your sentence comes to a full halt. This happens at every period. It also happens at every properly used colon and semicolon. (It can never happen at a comma, which (like this one) always forces us further into the sentence to find out just what kind of comma it was trying to be.) That full halt says to a reader, "Stress whatever is here." Where writing is concerned, nothing is more important than this to understand and control. It establishes a goal for your journey, a target for your vision. It is the same as building a lighthouse on a rocky shore. One's concentration is immediately focused on that lighthouse.

70

Place the words you want your reader to stress in a Stress position – just before a colon, semi-colon, or period. @GeoGopen

_____

_____

_____

71

"Stress position": A reader begins stressing words as soon as the reader believes there's nothing left but what's now beginning. @GeoGopen

_____

_____

_____

72

Linguist's definition of "Stress position":
A Stress position is any moment of full
syntactic closure. @GeoGopen

_____

_____

_____

73

Simple definition of "Stress position":
A Stress position is any moment the
grammatical structure comes to a full halt.
@GeoGopen

_____

_____

_____

74

The #1 tip for writing: Place stress-worthy
information in Stress positions – just before
colons, semicolons, or periods. @GeoGopen

_____

_____

_____

75

A main clause that ends with no colon, semicolon, or period causes serious trouble for a reader, who must guess what to stress.
@GeoGopen

_____

_____

_____

76

A sentence is too long when it has more viable candidates for Stress positions than it has colons, semicolons, or periods. @GeoGopen

_____

_____

_____

77

A sentence is too short when it has no viable candidate for a Stress position, indicated by a colon, semicolon, or period. @GeoGopen

_____

_____

_____

78

It may be natural for writers to front-load the important information in a sentence; but it is disastrous for readers. @GeoGopen

_____

_____

_____

79

The comma is the only punctuation mark that can't announce its function when it arrives. It therefore can't say "Stress this." @GeoGopen

_____

_____

_____

80

A comma can never create a Stress position:
It does not announce itself as a moment of
full syntactic closure. @GeoGopen

_____

_____

_____

81

You always have to keep reading beyond a comma to find out what kind of comma function it is trying to fulfill. @GeoGopen

_____

_____

_____

82

In a multi-clause sentence, readers try to give extra weight to the clause at the sentence's end. @GeoGopen

_____

_____

_____

83

In a multi-clause sentence, readers try to give extra weight to the sentence's main clause. @GeoGopen

---

84

Since anything at a colon, semicolon, or period invites emphasis, that's where you should put your most important stuff. @GeoGopen

---

85

Why "hide" your important stuff in places where the reader does not know to look for important stuff? (Most people hide it.) @GeoGopen

---

86

The #1 writing problem in the USA: Not placing words to be stressed next to a colon, semicolon, or period. @GeoGopen

---

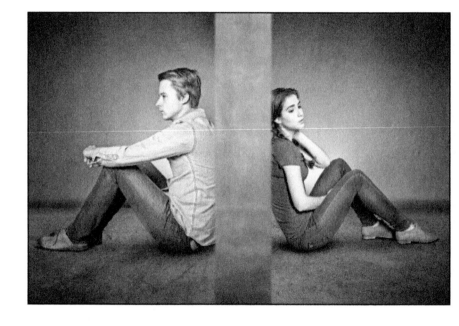

Section IX
Sentence Technicalities

Keep things that need to be together together. If they become separated, it causes the reader distress. A subject and its verb long to be together. In an infinitive, the word "to" and the verb form long to be together. Romeo and Juliet longed to be together. Look what trouble separating them caused. Location, location, location. Do not erect prison walls between elements of your sentence that desire a mutual embrace. Put things where they want to be, where they need to be.

87

Anything that intervenes between a subject and its verb is read by a reader as being less important – merely interruptive. @GeoGopen

_____

_____

_____

88

A subject and its verb should be close to one another in a sentence because their functions depend so critically on one another. @GeoGopen

_____

_____

_____

89

A subject and its verb lose touch with one another when too many words intervene between them. @GeoGopen

_____

_____

_____

90

A subject and its verb lose touch with one another when something intended for emphasis intervenes between them.
@GeoGopen

_____

_____

_____

91

Feel confident in locating short, easily read information between a subject and its verb if you want a reader not to emphasize it.
@GeoGopen

_____

_____

_____

92

Like many grammar rules, the split infinitive rule stemmed from our veneration of Latin, where the infinitive is unsplittable. @GeoGopen

_____

_____

_____

93

Feel free to boldly split your infinitive when writing for people that don't care about the split infinitive. Otherwise, don't. @GeoGopen

_____

_____

_____

94

By 2035, you will be able to split any infinitive you like. All the people who were trained to care will no longer be in power.
@GeoGopen

_____

_____

_____

95

A colon promises: The preceding clause will either be restated in different terms or be supported by a list of examples. @GeoGopen

_____

_____

_____

96

If a list is heavy-weight enough that each item requires emphasis, it should be introduced by a colon and divided by semi-colons. @GeoGopen

_____

_____

_____

97

If a list is light-weight enough to be read swiftly, it should be introduced by a double-dash and divided by commas. @GeoGopen

_____

_____

_____

98

Since a properly used colon produces a Stress position mid-sentence, it should be preceded by a full main clause. @GeoGopen

_____

_____

_____

99

Since a properly used semicolon produces a
Stress position mid-sentence , it should
be preceded by a full main clause.
@GeoGopen

_____

_____

_____

100

The semicolon as death: What comes
before stands alone as a unit, as does what
follows; but together the two make a whole.
@GeoGopen

_____

_____

_____

101

Parentheses that surround an interruptive comment in a sentence instruct the reader to ("lower the voice") within. @GeoGopen

---

102

Two double-dashes that surround an interruptive comment in a sentence instruct the reader to -- "Raise the Voice" -- within. @GeoGopen

---

103

The number of words in a sentence, taken by itself, is no indication of the sentence's quality. @GeoGopen

_____

_____

_____

104

A 130-word sentence can ring clear as a bell; and a 13-word sentence can be hopelessly opaque. The numbers don't matter. @GeoGopen

_____

_____

_____

105

A main clause that ends in anything other than a colon, semi-colon, or period is likely to prove burdensome to a reader. @GeoGopen

_____

_____

_____

106

Readers think a main clause – a clause that can stand by itself as a sentence – will contain the writer's main thought.
@GeoGopen

_____

_____

_____

107

The information in a dependent clause is considered by readers to be less important than the information in the main clause. @GeoGopen

_____

_____

_____

108

The information in a mere phrase is considered by readers to be less important than the information in a dependent clause. @GeoGopen

_____

_____

_____

109

The information in a mere phrase is considered by readers to be far less important than the information in the main clause. @GeoGopen

_____

_____

_____

110

Whenever an "and" connects two main clauses, it fails to tell a reader how to connect those clauses. Best avoid this structure. @GeoGopen

_____

_____

_____

Section X
Paragraphs

When you are engaged in the act of writing, no matter how large the document may be, your primary focus at any given moment is on the creation of a single sentence. For writers, the primary unit of discourse is the sentence. Not so for readers: For them, the primary unit of thought is the paragraph. They don't read paragraphs as a compilation of individual sentences, which they package together only after encountering them. They expect to be able to flow smoothly from sentence to sentence to sentence, as the thought of the paragraph slowly becomes revealed.

It therefore is important to know both how readers get from sentence to sentence, and how they expect whole paragraphs to be structured. What Miss Grundy taught us in the 7th grade won't work for writing as part of a professional life: Five brick-like sentences will not make a good paragraph. A good one needs not to be solid; it needs to be liquid. It must flow continuously from one sentence to the next. Or, if you prefer a solid simile, your paragraph must have inter-connecting parts that help it to move forward – just like cogs in a complex machine. I've written about paragraphs elsewhere, at more sufficient length.

111

The 5-sentence paragraph taught in school – topic sentence, body, conclusion – rarely exists in professional prose. Forget it. @GeoGopen

_____

_____

_____

112

Paragraphs have significant beginnings, middles, and ends, but no single, set structure that must be constantly reproduced. @GeoGopen

_____

_____

_____

113

For readers, a paragraph is not experienced as a series of separate sentences. Each sentence must flow into the next. @GeoGopen

_____

_____

_____

114

Each sentence in a paragraph will be understood not by itself, but only in the context made for it by the sentence before it. @GeoGopen

_____

_____

_____

115

The last sentence of a paragraph can on occasion be used effectively to say something witty, ironic, or even contradictory. @GeoGopen

_____

_____

_____

116

"Topic sentence"? A paragraph's first sentence cannot always fully inform readers what to expect from the paragraph as a whole. @GeoGopen

_____

_____

_____

117

Stating the issue at the beginning of a sophisticated paragraph can take one, two, or even three sentences. Four won't work. @GeoGopen

_____

_____

_____

118

In a paragraph, you never are sure the issue statement has finished until you know you are now launched into its discussion. @GeoGopen

_____

_____

_____

119

Readers appreciate a writer making a paragraph's point explicitly, in a single sentence, and located near the beginning or end. @GeoGopen

_____

_____

_____

120

Readers expect to find a paragraph's point up front, as the last sentence of the stated issue. Exception: 1st and last paragraphs. @GeoGopen

_____

_____

_____

121

For all opening paragraphs, readers expect the point to be announced at the end. @GeoGopen

_____

_____

_____

122

For all closing paragraphs, readers expect the point to be announced at the end.
@GeoGopen

_____

_____

_____

123

For 1st and last paragraphs, you can reserve your point for the end because you know most of your readers will still be with you.
@GeoGopen

_____

_____

_____

124

Narrative paragraphs – ("This happened. Then that.") – need not make a specific point. They help set up later points. @GeoGopen

_____

_____

_____

125

To see what readers will stress in your paragraph, underline a few words before every colon, semicolon, and period. Surprise! @GeoGopen

_____

_____

_____

126

In high school, the issue and point of a paragraph were usually the same, single sentence. Not so later on. @GeoGopen

_____

_____

_____

127

In a paragraph, the issue introduces the discussion; the point is the product or the cause of that discussion. @GeoGopen

_____

_____

_____

128

A one-sentence paragraph is fine if it states both the issue and the point of the paragraph and requires no discussion.
@GeoGopen

_____

_____

_____

129

A sentence presents a single thought; a paragraph presents and develops a single (perhaps multi-part) thought. @GeoGopen

_____

_____

_____

130

No matter what you are writing, most of your energy, at any given moment, is devoted to the construction of a single sentence. @GeoGopen

---

131

For writers, the primary unit of discourse is the sentence; for readers, the primary unit of thought is the paragraph. @GeoGopen

---

132

In a sentence, save the best for last; in most paragraphs (other than opening ones and closing ones), put first things first. @GeoGopen

_____

_____

_____

133

Like sentences, paragraphs connect backwards most securely by referencing either the beginning or the end of their predecessor. @GeoGopen

_____

_____

_____

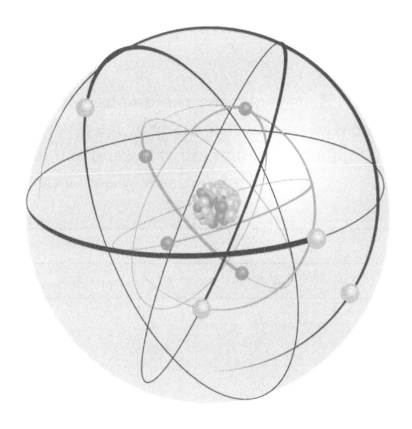

Section XI
Whole Documents

You might think that the structure of a whole document must be a good deal more complex than the structure of a sentence or paragraph. Not so – for two reasons: (1) The shape of professional documents is mandated by individual professions and is learned during one's apprenticeship. Lawyers eventually know where to state the facts, where to argue the law, and where to present the Issues Presented. Scientists know where to place the Methods, the Results, and the Discussion in a grant application or an article for publication. (2) A document is a long enough unit of discourse to allow the writer to articulate explicitly what its (unusual) structure is going to be. Even more than is the case for paragraphs, for documents one size (or shape) cannot fit all.

134

The gross structure of professional documents varies with each profession's needs and is usually learned on the job. @GeoGopen

_____

_____

_____

135

Articles on Science state their conclusions up front; those on Literature do it at the 3/4 mark. The difference matters. @GeoGopen

_____

_____

_____

136

The most rigid expectation: The last sentence of an opening paragraph promises the reader what the whole document will be about. @GeoGopen

_____

_____

_____

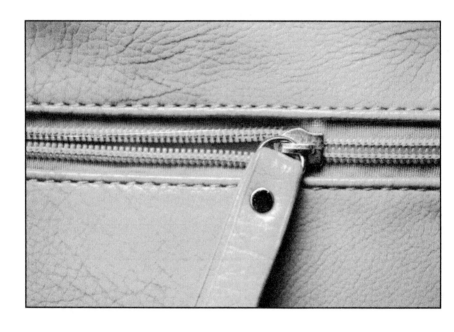

Section XII
In Closing

Closings should close.   The reader should have a feeling of "closing" while closing is happening. If you look at a picture of a zipper, how do you know if it is zipping or unzipping? You look at the zipper's pull-tab. In which direction is it leaning? That will tell you. Readers will know if you are pulling them towards closure. Once they sense that, they look forward to the closure of that closure. You can tell that the zipper is just about to complete its task. And the arrival at the end of a document – just like the arrival at the end of a sentence or a paragraph – carries with it a sense of completion, of fulfillment, of accomplishment. You have read and read, and now it is OVER. Arrival. Fulfillment. Completion. Or, as they used to indicate in movies in the 1920s, 1930s, and 1940s, THE END.

137

To discover whether you've had a thought –
and not just the impression that you've had
a thought – try to write it down.
@GeoGopen

_____

_____

_____

138

If you cannot express your thought in
writing, you probably have not yet finished
thinking it. @GeoGopen

_____

_____

_____

139

To learn more about Reader Expectations –
how readers go about making sense out of
prose – visit www.GeorgeGopen.com.
@GeoGopen

_____

_____

_____

140

To think better, write better. To write better,
know better how readers read: Learn to
understand their Reader Expectations.
@GeoGopen

_____

_____

_____

About the Author

George D. Gopen (J.D. and Ph.D., Harvard) is Professor Emeritus of the Practice of Rhetoric at Duke University, where he founded the University Writing Program and taught for 30 years. He is the 2011 recipient of the Legal Writing Institute's Golden Pen Award, a lifetime achievement award for contributions to the field of legal writing. His seminal article, "The Science of Scientific Writing," was selected by its publisher, *American Scientist*, as one of the 36 "Classic Articles" in the journal's 100 years of publication. It leads that journal's citation index. He is known worldwide for his Reader Expectations Approach to controlling the English language.

A m p l i f i e r™
Democratizing Thought Leadership

The Aha Amplifier™ is the only thought leadership platform with a built-in marketplace, making it easy to share curated content from like-minded thought leaders. There are over 25k diverse AhaMessages™ from thought leaders from around the world.

The Aha Amplifier makes it easy to create, organize, and share your own thought leadership AhaMessages in digestible, bite-sized morsels. Users are able to democratize thought leadership in their organizations by: 1) Making it easy for any advocate to share existing content with their Twitter, Facebook, LinkedIn & Google+ networks; 2) Allowing internal experts to create their own thought leadership content; and 3) Encouraging the expert's advocates to share that content on their networks.

The experience of many authors is that they have been able to create their social media-enabled AhaBooks™ of 140 AhaMessages in less than a day.

Sign up for a free account at
http://www.AhaAmplifier.com today!

Please pick up a copy of this book in the Aha Amplifier
and share each AhaMessage socially at
http://aha.pub/gopen

If you have reactions, questions, quibbles, or even complaints about the surface which has been scratched by these 140 nuggets of my Reader Expectation Approach to the language, please feel free to email me at **ggopen@duke.edu** or **george@george.gopen.com**. Also contact me if you want to write more persuasive grant applications, legal briefs, or any professional document that needs to achieve its goal. This new approach has already a long track record of success. One Duke University researcher/administrator, who failed AP English in high school, writes me that he has secured over $100,000,000 in grants since attending my faculty workshop in 1999.

CPSIA information can be obtained
at www.ICGtesting.com
Printed in the USA
BVOW07s2137150416

443989BV00009B/2/P